THE TOTALLY IRRESPONSIBLE SCIENCE KIT

SEAN CONNOLLY

WORKMAN PUBLISHING
NEW YORK

Library of Congress Cataloging-in-Publication Data is available.

ISBN 978-0-7611-8178-1

Workman books are available at special discounts when purchased in bulk for
premiums and sales promotions as well as for fund-raising or educational use.
Special editions or book excerpts can also be created to specification.
For details, contact the
Special Sales Director at the address below.

Mentos® is a registered trademark of
Perfetti Van Melle Benelux B.V. Corporation

WORKMAN is a registered trademark of
Workman Publishing Co., Inc.

Cover illustrations by Lou Brooks

Design by Robb Allen, Netta Rabin, and Phil Conigliaro
Illustrations by Lou Brooks and Robert James

Photo credits: **Fotolia:** BiterBig—pp. 42–43, 44–45 (blueprints); Goran
Bogicevic—p. 55 (sign); William Casey p. 39 (Chemist); Jeff Davies—
pp. 52–53 (cityscape); Christos Georghiou—pp. v, 43; Ruslan Grumble—
p. 47; Gudellaphoto—pp. 46–47 (rippling water). **Photofest/Universal
Pictures**—pp. 24, 25 (Frankenstein). **Shutterstock:** pp. 4 , 22–23 (potato),
27, 28, 33; Henk Bentlage—pp.13, 15 (cow); chippix—pp. 22 (child), 35;
Stephen Coburn—p. 26 ; Rafal Fabrykiewicz—pp. 12–13, 14–15 (clouds and
meadow); Andreas Gradin—p. 13 (house); Grebnev—p. 37 (bubbles);
Eric Isselee—p. 15 (pig); jet—pp. 12, 14 (rooster); Travis Manley—p. 2 (bottle);
Oligo— pp. 34–35 (bubbles); Photobank Gallery—pp. 8–9 (hands);
Diana Rich— pp. iv, vi, xi (robot); Ian Scott— pp. 4–5 James Steidl—
p. 10 (hand); Ross Strachan—pp. 30–31; Vinicius Tupinamba—
p. 12 (old woman).

Workman Publishing Co., Inc.
225 Varick Street
New York, NY 10014-4381
workman.com

Manufactured in China

First printing February 2015
10 9 8 7 6 5 4 3 2 1

To my companions on this wonderful journey—
Frederika, Jamie, Anna, Thomas, and Dafydd

CONTENTS

take me to
YOUR READER . . .

INTRODUCTION

The Oxford Dictionary of English defines science as "the intellectual and practical activity encompassing the systematic study of the structure and behavior of the physical and natural world through observation and experiment."

This definition explains the link between humankind's earliest paintings—with their vivid depictions of cave lions and predatory wolves—and the NASA space shuttle studies of atmospheric winds using laser radar. Through the ages, whether or not they called themselves "scientists," people have observed and experimented their way to a better understanding of the world and how it works.

Throughout our history, we have been driven by curiosity and the "need to know." Scientists have probed all manner of conundrums, teasing out answers and sharing their findings. Just think of how much of our knowledge can be traced to questions such as:

"Why does the sun rise and set every day?"

"Why did that ripe apple fall down from the tree and not up?"

"If water expands when it becomes steam, can it be used to drive a piston?"

"Can more than one computer be linked together using, say, a telephone connection?"

We know—or know how to find out—the answers to these and thousands of other questions that have inspired scientists through the ages. And we can see the benefits all around us, especially in the field of technology, which harnesses the advances of science and turns them to practical advantage.

NEW SETS OF QUESTIONS

The Totally Irresponsible Science Kit carries on this noble tradition of scientific exploration and takes it to new—yet, in many ways, familiar—areas. After all, the quest for knowledge does not end when we hang up our goggles and turn off the light in the science lab. The everyday world provides us with the tools to carry on with our scientific probing.

The 18 experiments described in the following pages use ingredients or materials found in most households or which can be easily bought. Like the classic scientific experiments, which use questions as launching pads for inquiry, these experiments also seek to find and demonstrate answers. Some of the answers, however, might well tie in with a completely different set of questions—along the lines of:

"What's that straw doing inside a potato?"

"Son, have you seen my bottle of diet cola?"

"What in the world has happened to this carnation?"

"Wait a minute! Why is there slime in the refrigerator?"

THE "I" WORD

All of this brings us to an important word in the title of this kit: *irresponsible*. Where does being irresponsible tie in with conducting experiments? Isn't it the opposite of the scientific method? Or is it possible that there could be more than one reading of the word *irresponsible*?

Kids, for instance, are always being labeled "irresponsible": by their parents because they don't clean their rooms, or walk their dogs, or keep their schoolwork neat and tidy. But for kids, these "responsible" duties simply get in the way of their "irresponsible" pursuits, like climbing trees or building sand castles. These activities, which are fueled by their curiosity and imagination, can be considered "irresponsible" to a certain degree, but it is exactly this definition of the "i" word that I wish to employ in this kit. By that definition, each of the experiments certainly does merit the descriptive term "irresponsible."

Although using the "i" word, *The Totally Irresponsible Science Kit* advocates due care and attention in each experiment. The presentation of each experiment is straightforward and logical, right down to any words of special warning that apply to the experiment. So please do take care when doing all these experiments.

WHO CAN DO THESE EXPERIMENTS?

The Totally Irresponsible Science Kit offers everyone, young or old, the chance to enter the fascinating world of science. For kids, who may just be entering this world, this kit offers the opportunity to witness firsthand the almost magical appeal of basic physics and chemistry. But while we hope for the active participation of budding young scientists whenever possible, these experiments should always be conducted under adult supervision. Bear in mind that the responsibility for each experiment lies with the adult supervising it. These experiments are *for* children as well as adults, but they are not to be conducted *by* children without adults.

The final section of each experiment, **Take Care!**, highlights any particular warnings relevant to the experiment. Some of these are no more than bits of friendly advice on how to get the best effects. Others have a more practical aim of drawing the reader's attention to ingredients or actions that call for extra care.

Apart from producing a result that will amuse, enchant, or possibly even inspire, each experiment is presented in a form that most of us recognize: a simple recipe.

HOW THIS KIT WORKS

The 18 entries in *The Totally Irresponsible Science Kit* represent different scientific themes or intended results.

A typical entry introduces the nature of the experiment and what to expect, before breaking it down into the following sections:

Time Factor: The time—from the first stage of preparation to the *oohs* and *aahs* at the conclusion—that it will take to perform this experiment. You might have a whole weekend free or only a few minutes to spare, so each experiment will have this handy guideline.

You Will Need: A straightforward list of ingredients.

Take Care! Special advice (and in some cases, warnings) for the experiment.

Method: Numbered step-by-step and easy-to-follow instructions.

The Scientific Excuse: The raison d'être for the experiment, or possibly your hurried explanation to an impatient or angry parent!

FINAL WORDS

So, isn't it time you went out and built that volcano you've always wanted to build? Or maybe you want to turn milk into stone? The following pages will let you do all of these things and much more, all in a spirit of playful scientific inquiry.

For most of the experiments, a broad smile and an open mind will count for far more than a white coat and a calculator. So throw yourself into these funny, eye-opening, quirky experiments and see where they take you. And in the process, you'll have a chance to learn—and maybe even teach others—a little science!

·*The*·
EXPERIMENTS

Cola GEYSER

SOME OF THE MOST MEMORABLE EXPERIMENTS CAN BE DONE with ingredients that don't seem in the least "scientific." For example, you can mix a popular candy and an even more popular soft drink to create your own version of Old Faithful. The volatile mixture sends a geyser as high as 20 feet.

chill, dude.

Don't forget to wear your goggles

You Will Need

- **1.32-OUNCE PACKAGE OF MENTOS CANDIES (ANY FLAVOR)**
- **VACUUMATIC TEST TUBE**
- **2-INCH-SQUARE PIECE OF CARDBOARD**
- **2-LITER PLASTIC BOTTLE OF DIET COLA**
- **PHOTON-REFRACTING GOGGLES**

TAKE CARE! DO THIS EXPERIMENT OUTDOORS, WELL AWAY FROM ANYTHING (OR ANYONE) YOU WOULDN'T WANT TO BECOME A STICKY WET MESS. UNLESS YOU WANT SOMETHING—OR SOMEONE—TO BECOME A STICKY WET MESS, IN WHICH CASE YOU SHOULD PERFORM THIS EXPERIMENT AT YOUR OWN RISK!

METHOD

1. Put 12 Mentos candies in the test tube and hold the cardboard to the open top of the tube.

2. Open the bottle of diet cola and put the test tube upside down on top of the open bottle, still holding the cardboard in place.

3. Take care to know which way to run.

4. Slide the cardboard away quickly so that the candies drop in.

5. Run clear and watch as the cola explodes out of the bottle.

The Scientific Excuse

This explosive reaction comes from the sudden release of carbon dioxide, the gas that gives soda its bubbles. This carbon dioxide normally remains dissolved in the soda because there are no nucleation sites—irregularities around which bubbles can form. Seen close up, a single Mento has a craggy surface—providing hundreds of nucleation sites. A dozen of those candies dumped in at once sets off a massive release of carbon dioxide, forcing the cola out of the bottle like a rocket. Diet cola works best because most non-diet colas use corn syrup, which suppresses the formation of bubbles.

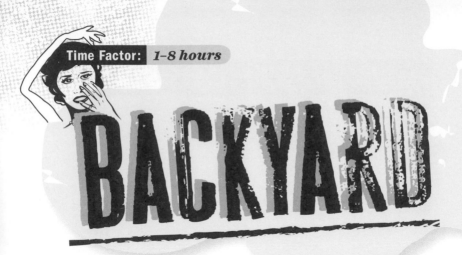

BACKYARD

THIS VIVID DISPLAY OF A CHEMICAL REACTION ISN'T dangerous, but it earns its place in this book by being very, very messy. It goes without saying that this is an outdoor experiment, so make sure you choose a dry (low humidity) day to demonstrate those dramatic lava flows. And if you're feeling really resourceful, you can add some to-scale model houses at the base of the volcano.

You Will Need

- EMPTY 1-LITER BOTTLE (GLASS OR PLASTIC)
- 3 SQUARE SHEETS OF PLYWOOD
- MODELING CLAY OR PAPIER-MÂCHÉ (ENOUGH TO FORM A "VOLCANIC CONE" ABOUT 13 INCHES ACROSS AT ITS BASE)
- LATERAL SPLIT-ORB MEASURING SPOON
- 3 TEASPOONS BAKING SODA
- 2 TEASPOONS DISHWASHING LIQUID
- RED OR YELLOW FOOD COLORING
- MATTER-RETAINING MEASURING CUP
- 1/4 CUP VINEGAR
- PHOTON-REFRACTING GOGGLES

Don't forget to wear your goggles

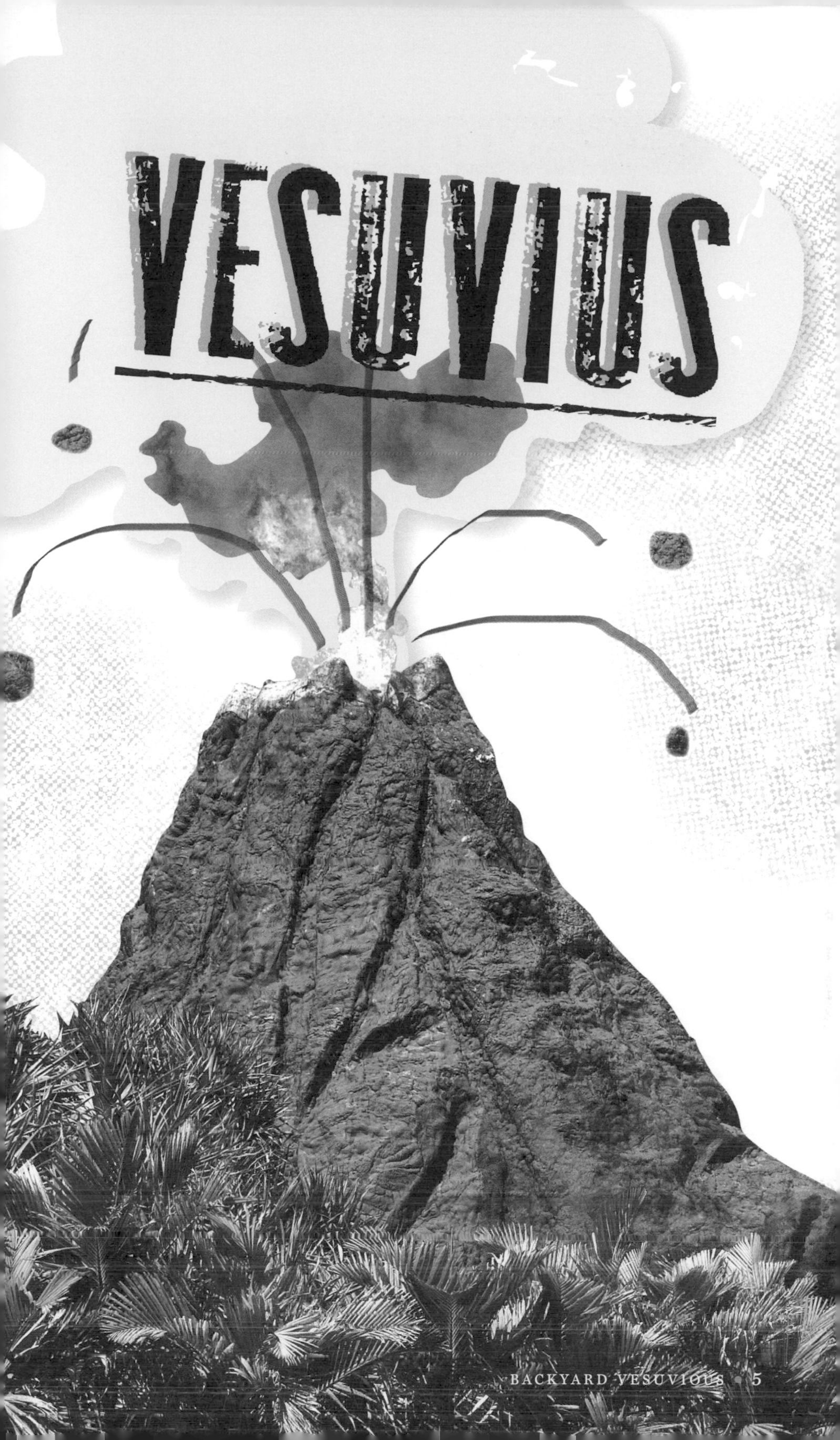
VESUVIUS

METHOD

1 Put the empty bottle in the middle of the sheet of plywood. It will be the center of the volcano.

2 Build the volcano around this bottle, using either modeling clay or papier-mâché.

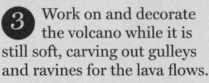

3 Work on and decorate the volcano while it is still soft, carving out gulleys and ravines for the lava flows.

TAKE CARE! THE BIGGEST PROBLEM WITH THIS EXPERIMENT IS THE POSSIBLE MESS, BUT GIVING TOO MUCH OF A WARNING HERE WOULD BE OVERDOING IT, WOULDN'T IT? BESIDES, WHAT'S A VOLCANO WITHOUT A LITTLE MESS?

4 Make sure the finished volcano has enough time to dry.

5 Add the baking soda, dishwashing liquid, and a squirt of food coloring to the empty bottle.

6 Put on the goggles.

7 Pour the vinegar into the bottle.

8 Stand back as the forces of nature take over!

Boom!

The Scientific Excuse

The trigger for the eruption is the addition of the vinegar (an acid) to the earlier mixture, which is basic (the opposite of acidic) thanks to the inclusion of baking soda. Adding the vinegar triggers an "acid/base neutralization," as chemists would put it. More specifically, this reaction changes carbonic acid into water and carbon dioxide; the liberated carbon dioxide leads to the dramatic foaming

HOMEMADE

WHAT'S WEATHER TALK WITHOUT A LITTLE EXAGGERATION now and then? Okay, well, maybe real lightning is a few trillion times more powerful, but this experiment goes right to the heart of the science that produces a lightning bolt—an electrical discharge. In the case of real lightning, this discharge goes from cloud to cloud. Here, the distance and scale are more modest—the breadth of a fingernail. But with the lights out and a good explanation, this can be a real crowd-pleaser—especially if you enlist the help of a younger brother or sister. "Hey, Mom, do you mind if I drop a little lightning bolt on Jack? Thanks!"

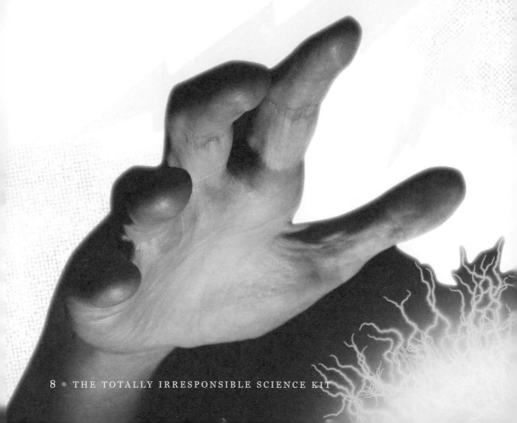

LIGHTNING

You Will Need

- THUMBTACK
- ALUMINUM-FOIL PIE PLATE
- BALLPOINT PEN

- GLUE, IF NEEDED
- 12-INCH X 4-INCH X 1-INCH STYROFOAM BLOCK
- WOOL SOCK

METHOD

1 Push the thumbtack from the back of the pie plate through the center.

2 Press the non-writing end of the pen into the tack point, securing with glue if needed.

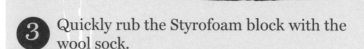

3 Quickly rub the Styrofoam block with the wool sock.

TAKE CARE! THE FOLLOWING IS NOT A SAFETY WARNING (THIS IS ONE OF THE SAFEST EXPERIMENTS IN THE KIT). FILE IT INSTEAD UNDER "FOLLOW THIS ADVICE IF YOU WANT THE EXPERIMENT TO WORK." MAKE SURE YOU ARE HOLDING THE PEN WHEN YOU PLACE THE PIE PLATE ON THE STYROFOAM. OTHERWISE, THE EXCESS ELECTRONS WILL FLOW UNDRAMATICALLY FROM STYROFOAM TO PIE PLATE TO FINGER.

4 Using the pen as a handle, pick up the pie plate (not touching the plate itself).

5 Put the pie plate down carefully on the Styrofoam.

6 Turn out the lights. Draw your finger closer and closer to the pie plate.

7 You should see, hear, and feel a small spark.

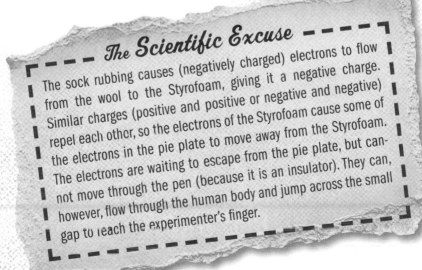

ZAP!

The Scientific Excuse

The sock rubbing causes (negatively charged) electrons to flow from the wool to the Styrofoam, giving it a negative charge. Similar charges (positive and positive or negative and negative) repel each other, so the electrons of the Styrofoam cause some of the electrons in the pie plate to move away from the Styrofoam. The electrons are waiting to escape from the pie plate, but cannot move through the pen (because it is an insulator). They can, however, flow through the human body and jump across the small gap to reach the experimenter's finger.

HEAVY WEATHER?

GLOBAL WARMING, CARBON EMISSIONS, THE OZONE LAYER—it can all seem a little baffling, especially for young people with relatively little science background. But given a chance to create some carbon dioxide—and then see how it's a force to be reckoned with—you might want to learn a little more about carbon offsetting. Plus, there's always something spooky about invisible forces at work around us. Build yourself a homemade scale to prove that the invisible carbon dioxide is heavier than the equally invisible air.

You Will Need

- THUMBTACK
- TABLE
- TAPE
- 2 CLEAR PLASTIC BAGS (SANDWICH-BAG SIZE)
- 12-INCH RULER
- MATTER-RETAINING MEASURING CUP
- ½ CUP VINEGAR
- DRINKING GLASS
- 3 TEASPOONS BAKING SODA
- LATERAL SPLIT-ORB MEASURING SPOON

METHOD

1. Place the thumbtack pointing up near the corner of the table.

2. Tape an open plastic bag (leaving a good upward-facing opening) to each end of the ruler.

3. Carefully balance the ruler on the thumbtack point to create a homemade scale.

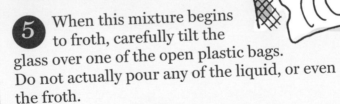

4. Pour the vinegar into the drinking glass. Add the baking soda.

5. When this mixture begins to froth, carefully tilt the glass over one of the open plastic bags. Do not actually pour any of the liquid, or even the froth.

6. The bag beneath the glass should slowly sink under the weight of the invisible new ingredient.

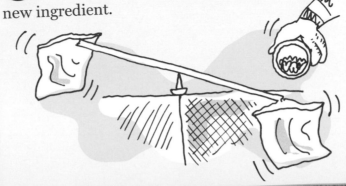

TAKE CARE! TILT THE GLASS GENTLY ONCE YOU HAVE ADDED THE BAKING SODA TO THE VINEGAR. HAVING GONE TO THE TROUBLE OF CREATING THE DELICATE SCALE, YOU DON'T WANT TO BLOW THE EXPERIMENT BY POURING THE LIQUID INTO THE BAG—THE WHOLE POINT IS THAT THE BAG IS DRAGGED DOWN BY THE INVISIBLE GAS!

The Scientific Excuse

A diligent science student will recognize that mixing vinegar and baking soda is one of the best—and easiest—ways of producing carbon dioxide. Carbon dioxide is a by-product of the reaction between an acid (vinegar) and a base (baking soda). Moreover, carbon dioxide is heavier than air. That's why it can be poured, just as one could pour a liquid into one of the bags, causing the scale to tip.

Static Electricity SLIME

THIS IS ONE OF THE BEST EXPERIMENTS FOR YOUNGER scientists. It's very messy, and the seemingly risky combination of ooze and electricity makes for a good show.

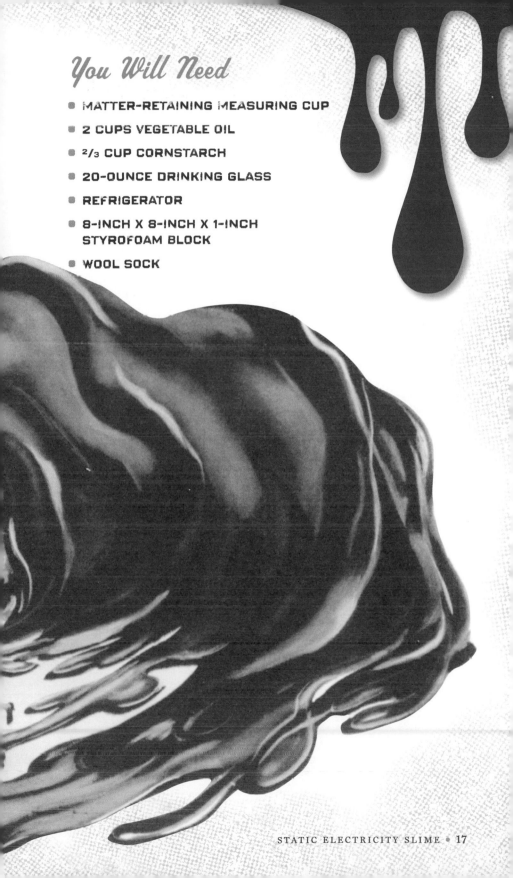

You Will Need

- MATTER-RETAINING MEASURING CUP
- 2 CUPS VEGETABLE OIL
- $2/3$ CUP CORNSTARCH
- 20-OUNCE DRINKING GLASS
- REFRIGERATOR
- 8-INCH X 8-INCH X 1-INCH STYROFOAM BLOCK
- WOOL SOCK

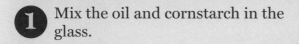

METHOD

1 Mix the oil and cornstarch in the glass.

2 Put this mixture in the refrigerator until it's well chilled.

3 Remove from the refrigerator and stir (don't worry if it has separated).

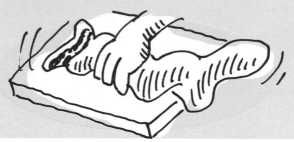

4 Let the mixture warm up enough so that it can flow; it will resemble slime at this point.

5 When the mixture is ready, rub the Styrofoam block on the wool sock (or on your hair if there's no wool sock handy).

TAKE CARE! **THIS IS ONE OF THOSE RARE EXPERIMENTS THAT'S SAFE ENOUGH TO RECOMMEND EVEN TO YOUR KID BROTHER OR SISTER. JUST REMEMBER TO MAKE SURE THAT THE GLASS IS BIG ENOUGH TO HOLD THE OIL-CORNSTARCH MIXTURE.**

6 Tip the container of slime and put the electrically charged Styrofoam about an inch away from it. The slime should seem to stop flowing, and even to gel.

7 Try wiggling the Styrofoam: Bits of slime might break off and follow it.

8 You can refrigerate the slime in a sealed container after the experiment.

BRRR

The Scientific Excuse

When rubbed, the Styrofoam draws electrons from the wool (or hair), giving the Styrofoam a negative charge. Meanwhile, the oil and cornstarch combine to make a substance known as a colloid. In school, we learn that there are three forms of matter: solid, liquid, and gas. But there's actually a fourth kind of matter—a colloid—that is neither a solid nor a liquid, although it has characteristics of both. When the charged Styrofoam nears the colloid, it causes the cornstarch to line up, blocking the flow of the liquid oil. Taking the Styrofoam away lets the mixture behave more a like a normal liquid again.

Burning ICE

LIGHTING A FIRE WITH A BLOCK OF ICE? SURELY THAT'S A contradiction in terms! Try this experiment to see for yourself how the forces of nature can overturn common sense. It's certainly one display you and your audience won't easily forget.

You Will Need

- SAUCEPAN
- WATER
- SHALLOW, EVENLY CURVED PLASTIC BOWL (ABOUT 8 INCHES WIDE)
- ENOUGH ROOM ON A FREEZER SHELF FOR THE BOWL
- BLACK CREPE PAPER
- FLAMEPROOF PLATE
- SUNLIGHT

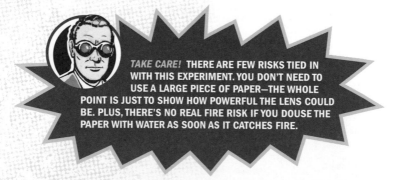

TAKE CARE! THERE ARE FEW RISKS TIED IN WITH THIS EXPERIMENT. YOU DON'T NEED TO USE A LARGE PIECE OF PAPER—THE WHOLE POINT IS JUST TO SHOW HOW POWERFUL THE LENS COULD BE. PLUS, THERE'S NO REAL FIRE RISK IF YOU DOUSE THE PAPER WITH WATER AS SOON AS IT CATCHES FIRE.

METHOD

1 Boil a saucepan of water for 3–4 minutes and then let it cool to just above room temperature.

2 Fill the bowl with the previously boiled water.

3 Carefully place the bowl of water on a shelf in the freezer and allow it to freeze completely.

4 Scrunch up a small piece of the crepe paper and set it on a flameproof plate.

5 Remove the ice from the bowl (running a little warm water over the back of the bowl can help to release it).

6 Hold the ice, which is shaped like a lens, above the paper and direct the sunlight at the paper.

7 Keep the ice still until the paper ignites.

The Scientific Excuse

This experiment operates under the same principle as letting a magnifying glass light an object: It concentrates, or refracts, the sunlight and focuses it on the paper. The ice has very little chance of cooling these rays. And boiling the water first is important as a way of "purifying" the lens. Ordinary water has many bubbles inside it: Even the ones too small for us to see can distort the lens and make it less effective.

POTATO GUN

T HIS EXPERIMENT TAKES THE NOTION OF A FOOD FIGHT and introduces a note of the "arms race." The basic ammunition is simple enough—the humble potato. But with a little preparation, and some help from Boyle's Law, the potato will "go ballistic"—literally!

You Will Need

- 2 POTATOES
- 4-FOOT LENGTH OF PVC PIPE (1-INCH DIAMETER), AVAILABLE AT MOST HARDWARE STORES
- PHOTON-REFRACTING GOGGLES
- 5-FOOT WOODEN BROOMSTICK (DIAMETER NARROWER THAN THAT OF THE PIPE)
- RUBBER STOPPER (OPTIONAL)

The Scientific Excuse

This experiment is an explosive demonstration of Boyle's Law: Pressure increases as volume decreases. Scientifically stated, this means: "Under constant temperature, the volume of a gas is inversely proportional to the total amount of pressure applied." In this experiment, the gas is the air inside the pipe, lodged between the two potato plugs. When you shove the broomstick into the pipe, you push one plug toward the other. This suddenly reduces the volume of the gas, thereby increasing its pressure. Something has to give: The burst of pressure sends the potato plug flying.

METHOD

1 Press one end of the pipe down into a potato, so that a plug of potato becomes lodged in the end.

2 Repeat this process with the other potato in the other end of the pipe so that you have a potato plug at each end.

Don't forget to wear your goggles.

3 Put on the goggles. With one hand, hold the pipe with one end pointing away from you—and anything breakable.

4 Position the broomstick at the closer end of the pipe, just touching the potato plug. (If the broomstick is much narrower than the pipe, add a rubber stopper to the end touching the potato.)

5 Edge the broomstick slowly down the pipe, pushing one potato plug toward the other. Stop when you are about a third of the way down, and pull the broomstick back.

6 Now, ram the broomstick back into the pipe very quickly. The plug at the far ("barrel") end will shoot out with great force.

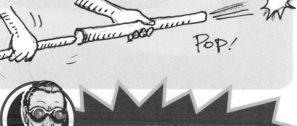

POP!

TAKE CARE! DON'T POINT THE POTATO GUN IN THE DIRECTION OF ANYONE WATCHING—OR TOWARD ANY CHINA OR GLASS! IT'S BETTER, ALL THINGS CONSIDERED, TO DO THIS EXPERIMENT OUTSIDE.

FRANKENSTEIN'S HAND

HERE'S A "HANDS-ON" DEMONSTRATION of a scientific principle that has cropped up elsewhere in this book: the chemical reaction between a common acid and an equally familiar base. You can give this experiment something of a Halloween flavor by marking the glove with bones, veins, and screws. You can also add a little ketchup at the bottom of the glove—just to raise the gore factor. Your audience will love the special effects as the hand grows and grows.

You Will Need

- LATERAL SPLIT-ORB MEASURING SPOON
- 9 TEASPOONS VINEGAR
- DRINKING GLASS
- 2 TEASPOONS BAKING SODA
- RUBBER GLOVE

TAKE CARE! THIS IS A SAFE EXPERIMENT WITH VERY LITTLE RISK. MAKE SURE THAT THE GLOVE FITS TIGHTLY ON THE GLASS BEFORE YOU DO THE EXPERIMENT; IF IT'S LOOSE, TRY A WIDER-MOUTHED GLASS. YOU MIGHT WANT TO TAKE CARE THAT THE GLOVE DOESN'T INFLATE TOO MUCH, WHICH COULD CAUSE IT TO FLY OFF THE GLASS. AND IN CASE YOU'RE THINKING ABOUT HAVING A LITTLE FUN AT YOUR LITTLE BROTHER'S OR SISTER'S EXPENSE—SAY, BY TELLING HIM OR HER YOU FOUND THIS HAND ON THE SIDEWALK—DON'T COME RUNNING TO US IF YOU GET IN TROUBLE WITH THE PARENTAL UNITS!

METHOD

kinda stinks . . .

1 Pour the vinegar into the glass.

2 Add the baking soda to the inside of the glove. Hold the glove by its wrist and shake the powder into the fingers.

3 Carefully attach the glove to the top of the glass as shown so there's no gap.

4 Pull the glove upright by its fingertips and shake gently, allowing the baking soda to drop into the glass.

5 Stand back and watch as Frankenstein's hand begins to come alive.

It's alive!

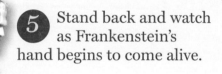

The Scientific Excuse

Baking soda is a chemical base, which reacts strongly with the acetic acid of the vinegar. One of the by-products of this reaction is carbon dioxide, which increases the pressure inside the glove-glass arrangement. As more gas is produced, the pressure increases further and pushes out the weaker surface (the rubber glove), inflating it gently.

Turning MILK TO STONE

THERE'S SOMETHING ALMOST MAGICAL IN THE TITLE OF THIS experiment, but once you've done it and understand what's happened, you'll also be reminded of Little Miss Muffet. Regardless of which reference you prefer (maybe none at all), this demonstration scores high on the "kewl" and "awesome" scale.

You Will Need

- MATTER-RETAINING MEASURING CUP
- 1½ CUPS SKIM MILK
- MICROWAVE-SAFE MIXING BOWL
- LATERAL SPLIT-ORB MEASURING SPOON
- 4 TEASPOONS VINEGAR
- MICROWAVE OVEN
- STRAINER
- EMPTY MILK CONTAINER

TAKE CARE! MAKE SURE YOU USE THE MICROWAVE RESPONSIBLY. OTHERWISE, THIS EXPERIMENT IS HAZARD-FREE. (UNLESS WHOEVER POURED THEMSELVES A CUP OF "STONE" DIDN'T APPRECIATE THE HUMOR!)

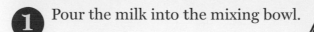

METHOD

1 Pour the milk into the mixing bowl.

2 Add the vinegar.

3 Put the bowl in the microwave and cook it on high for 1 minute.

4 Remove the bowl from the microwave to find a mixture that is now composed of a solid and a liquid.

5 Strain off the liquid.

6 Let the solid cool and then form it into little shapes, which will harden as they cool.

7 Put the shapes into the empty milk container, and put the container in the refrigerator. Next time someone goes for a nice refreshing cup of milk, won't they be surprised to find weird, hard little shapes inside instead?

The Scientific Excuse

The acid in the vinegar separates the curd (the semi-solid element) from the whey (the liquid) in the milk. The protein in the curd accounts for its rubbery quality—in fact, some of the earliest plastics were produced in a variation of this experiment.

ROSES ARE RED?

CLEVER FLORISTS MANAGE TO GET GREEN CARNATIONS FOR Saint Patrick's Day each year. Did you ever wonder how? Here's your chance to get in on the secret.

You Will Need

- **2 FOUNTAIN PEN INK CARTRIDGES (1 RED AND 1 GREEN)**
- **2 VACUUMATIC TEST TUBES**
- **WATER**
- **SHARP KNIFE**
- **WHITE-BLOSSOM FLOWER (E.G., ROSE OR CARNATION) WITH A 6- TO 8-INCH STEM**
- **10-OUNCE DRINKING GLASS**

TAKE CARE! **MAKE SURE THE SPLIT PART OF THE STEM IS MAINLY SUBMERGED SINCE IT COULD ALLOW TOO MUCH AIR IN OTHERWISE, KILLING THE PLANT AND RUINING YOUR EXPERIMENT.**

METHOD

1 Pour each ink cartridge into a separate test tube.

2 Dilute the ink by half filling each tube with water.

3 With a knife, carefully slit the stem of the flower so that its base has 2 halves, each as long as a test tube. The stem should remain whole above the slit.

4 Put a stem half in each test tube and place the tubes (still holding the stem) inside the glass.

5 Keep the tubes upright for several hours.

6 The blossom will have changed color gradually—one part becoming red and the other part turning green.

The Scientific Excuse

The diluted ink is mainly water, which the plant needs for nourishment. It travels through the narrow channels that transport water and nutrients to the different parts of a plant. The coloring (in reality, tiny particles of solid) hits the end of the line when it reaches the blossom, although the accompanying water either is used by the plant or evaporates from the surface of the blossom. What remains is the distinct color.

DO-IT-YOURSELF
BLUBBER

POLAR BEARS, WHALES, AND SEALS CAN LIVE MOST OF THEIR lives in subfreezing air or near-freezing waters, yet each of these species is a mammal. And mammals are warm-blooded creatures that need to create and preserve heat in order to survive. Here's a chance to experience the secret of these Arctic survivors. This secret is called "blubber."

You Will Need

- MATTER-RETAINING MEASURING CUP
- 1 CUP VEGETABLE OIL
- 4 ZIPLOCK SANDWICH BAGS
- MASKING TAPE
- SINK OR DEEP BUCKET
- COLD WATER AND ICE CUBES
- TIMER (OR WATCH WITH A SECOND HAND)

METHOD

1. Add the vegetable oil to an open sandwich bag.

2. Turn a second sandwich bag inside out and insert it in the first bag.

3. Zip the inside bag to the outside bag so that the cooking oil is between them.

4. Tape shut any gaps where the bags join.

5. Connect the other 2 sandwich bags together in the same way, only without any oil. (Each pair of bags becomes a "mitten.")

6. Fill the sink or bucket with cold water and add some ice cubes to lower the temperature further.

7. Put a mitten on each hand, start the timer, and submerge your hands in the cold water.

8. Time how long you can keep each mittened hand—"blubber" and normal—in the water before you have to pull one out because your hand has become too cold.

The Scientific Excuse

The key to survival in very cold temperatures is preserving body heat. Blubber, the thick layer of fat under the skin of whales and seals, does that by insulating the body. In effect, it blocks the flow of heat from the body to the outside. In this experiment, the oil (petroleum jelly would work as well if you had enough of it) insulates your hand in the same way.

THE *Bubble* CHILD

EVERYONE, YOUNG AND OLD, HAS BLOWN BUBBLES, SO THERE doesn't seem much more that can be said about them. But imagine how your most "been there, done that" friend would feel about actually being engulfed in a bubble. This is a great warm weather experiment to perform outdoors. Have a camera ready to record the outcome since there are bound to be doubters when you—or your friend—describe the result. The "secret ingredient" (glycerin) adds color and strength to the bubbles.

TAKE CARE! MAKE SURE THE BUBBLE SOLUTION IS KEPT FROM YOUR FRIEND'S EYES—WEAR YOUR *GOGGLES* AS A GOOD PRECAUTION. ALSO BEAR IN MIND THAT THE QUALITY OF BUBBLE VARIES WITH THE TYPE OF WATER BEING USED (SOME WATER HAS NATURALLY OCCURRING MINERALS THAT MAKE IT A BIT HARDER TO DO THE EXPERIMENT). IT'S ALSO BEST TO TRY THIS EXPERIMENT WHEN THE WEATHER IS HUMID.

You Will Need

- MATTER-RETAINING MEASURING CUP
- 2 CUPS DISHWASHING LIQUID
- 3 CUPS TAP WATER
- ½ CUP GLYCERIN (SOLD AT MOST PHARMACIES)
- 2-GALLON BUCKET (IDEALLY WITH LID)
- SMALL WADING POOL (MINIMUM 3-FOOT DIAMETER)
- PLASTIC HULA HOOP
- SMALL STOOL
- PHOTON-REFRACTING GOGGLES

Don't forget to wear your goggles.

1 Pour the dishwashing liquid, water, and glycerin into the bucket and mix to make the bubble mixture. (This mixture can keep—and even improves over time— but you must cover the bucket.)

2 Pour the bubble mixture into the pool.

3 Place the hula hoop in the pool so it's immersed in the solution.

4 Taking care not to puncture the base of the pool, place the stool inside the hula hoop.

5 Ask a friend to put on the goggles and stand on the stool—it's always best to choose someone who likes to be thought of as cool, to watch the transformation.

6 Lift the hula hoop up and over your friend: A giant bubble will engulf him or her.

The Scientific Excuse

The dishwashing liquid (soap) is the prime ingredient for any blown bubble. Each soap molecule has two halves—one hydrophilic (attracted to water) and one hydrophobic (repelled by water). The bubble is actually a "sandwich": a layer of water molecules squeezed between two layers of soap molecules. The two enemies of bubbles are water tension and evaporation. The interaction with the soap molecules stretches the water molecules apart, weakening the tension. The other ingredient, glycerin, forms weak hydrogen bonds with the water, slowing or even preventing evaporation.

Magical ATOM

THIS EXPERIMENT ALMOST SEEMS TO BE A MAGIC TRICK— surely adding one cup of rubbing alcohol to one cup of water gives us two cups of that combined liquid? Actually, the answer is no, because some of the alcohol molecules find their way into spaces between the water molecules. It's a bit like adding a cup of water to a cup of marbles.

You Will Need

- MATTER-RETAINING MEASURING CUP
- WATER
- 2-PINT CLEAR GLASS CONTAINER (WITH FRACTIONS OF CUPS MARKED ON IT)
- PHOTON-REFRACTING GOGGLES
- ISOPROPYL (RUBBING) ALCOHOL

Don't forget to wear your goggles.

The Scientific Excuse

If you could miniaturize yourself down to the scale of atoms and molecules (groups of atoms held together chemically), you'd see real differences in their sizes. That means that you'd see larger gaps between some of them (imagine a group of basketballs) than you'd notice between others (bunches of sand). In this experiment, the alcohol is playing the part of the sand, filling the gaps between water molecules (basketballs).

METHOD

1 Carefully measure 1 cup of water and pour it into the 2-pint container. (Your measurements must be exact for the experiment to work.)

2 Put on the goggles.

3 Carefully measure 1 cup of rubbing alcohol and add it to the water. Again, be exact!

4 Now take a precise reading of the amount of liquid in the container. It should come to less than 2 cups (1 pint).

TAKE CARE! **DON'T LET ANY SMALL CHILDREN NEAR THE RUBBING ALCOHOL, AND MAKE SURE YOU WEAR THE GOGGLES TO PROTECT YOUR EYES FROM SPLASHES WHEN YOU POUR IN THE ALCOHOL.**

MOLECULE

THIS EXPERIMENT SHOWS THAT MOLECULES ARE MOVING around even if we can't see them. A few drops of food coloring will simply remain little blobs of strong color in clear water unless you stir them in, right? Well, the water molecules themselves will probably do all that stirring themselves if you give them time—just remember that Brownian Motion.

You Will Need

- WATER
- GLASS JAR (ABOUT 12–16 FLUID OUNCES)
- FOOD COLORING

TAKE CARE! MAKE SURE YOU CHOOSE A DARK FOOD COLORING BECAUSE IT HIGHLIGHTS THE DRAMATIC PAYOFF BETTER.

MADNESS

METHOD

1 Fill the jar about halfway with water.

2 Add several drops of food coloring. They should be clearly visible as a darker color even as they sink to the bottom.

3 Leave the jar still for 3 hours.

4 Observe the liquid again—it should be all one color, as if the food coloring had been stirred in.

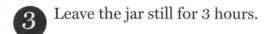

The Scientific Excuse

The great Albert Einstein was fascinated by Brownian Motion—how molecules move around randomly all the time. It's named for Robert Brown, a Scottish scientist who first observed pollen grains moving in a clear liquid even though they weren't being shaken or stirred. The water molecules in this experiment move in that same way, constantly bumping one another and into the food coloring molecules. Those crashes spread the food coloring molecules around just as if you had stirred them.

Soda Bottle
ROCKET

THIS EXPERIMENT GIVES YOU A CHANCE TO BUILD A ROCKET with liquid fuel—well, sort of. And it is as good a test of Newton's third law as any space flight.

TAKE CARE! **THE ROCKET CAN GO OFF AT AN ANGLE, SO YOU *MUST* HAVE A CAR OR WALL AS A BARRIER BETWEEN YOU AND THE ROCKET.**

The Scientific Excuse

Need reminding about Isaac Newton's third law of motion? It tells us that "for every action, there is an equal and opposite reaction." This rocket launch is a good example. Your pumping has increased the pressure of the air inside the bottle. Eventually, there's enough pressure on the water to blast the cork off (the "action"). But that action has an equally powerful "reaction" in the opposite direction—the rocket blasting off.

You Will Need

- EMPTY 2-LITER SODA BOTTLE
- SCISSORS
- STIFF CARDBOARD
- SCOTCH TAPE
- HAMMER
- NAIL
- CORK STOPPER (LIKE THE KIND IN A WINE BOTTLE) TO FIT SNUGLY INTO THE SODA BOTTLE MOUTH

- ADAPTER PIN FOR INFLATING BASKETBALLS OR FOOTBALLS
- 8 FEET OF PLASTIC TUBING (FROM HARDWARE STORE): TAKE BIKE PUMP TO STORE AND CHOOSE TUBING THAT FITS EASILY INTO THE PUMP
- WATER
- BIKE FLOOR PUMP (UPRIGHT)

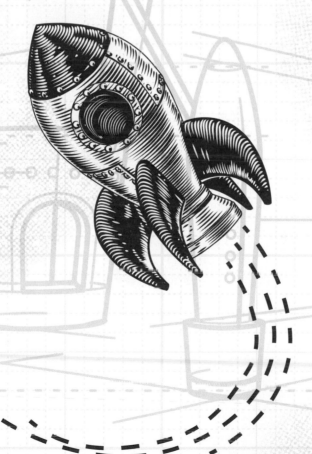

METHOD

1. The "rocket" will be the empty bottle, turned upside down, so the first step will be to add cardboard fins to raise the mouth of the bottle about 3 inches off the ground.

2. Cut 3 pieces of cardboard to make the fins. They should have a flat edge that can be taped onto the side of the bottle and a flat (not pointed) base so the bottle can rest on them.

3. Tape on the fins and test the bottle to see whether it will stand upright. Make alterations if necessary.

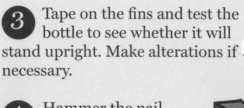

4. Hammer the nail through the center of the cork to make a hole. Then slide the adapter pin through the hole so it comes all the way through to the other side of the cork. The adapter pin should fit snugly inside.

5 Connect the end of the adapter with one end of the plastic tubing. This will give you a distance of 8 feet between you and the rocket during liftoff.

You must stand behind a protective barrier, such as a wall or a parked car, positioned between you and the rocket.

6 Fill the bottle ⅓ full of water and then fit the cork in snugly; the other end is in place at the pump.

7 Turn the rocket over very gently so that it stands upright.

8 Make sure everyone is as far away from the liftoff site as possible. **Make sure whoever is pumping the bicycle pump is behind the protective barrier.**

9 Pump steadily: The pressure builds up inside the bottle until it blows off the stopper and launches.

Chain REACTION

THIS EXPERIMENT DOESN'T INVOLVE RADIOACTIVITY, BUT IT is a good way to get you to think about chain reactions. It is also one of the easiest, hardest, strangest, funniest, quickest, most time-consuming experiments in the whole kit—depending on your point of view and what you make of it. But before you read ahead, remember that whatever you do is meant to help you understand the idea of a chain reaction. And a chain reaction is pretty much just what it says. It involves a series of steps or stages that are connected in some way.

For example, you could set up a chain reaction that begins with letting a marble go down a ramp set up on an ironing board until it rolls into a plastic cup on the edge, which gets knocked off the ironing board but is tied to the board with a string so it swings into a row of dominoes, and then the last domino falls and . . . well, you get the picture.

It all boils down to using your own imagination—and as many things as the nearest grown-ups will let you borrow. Just remember that you can't use any plug-in electrical item (battery-operated toys are okay, though) and you shouldn't set the experiment up so that anything valuable could break.

You Will Need

- IRONING BOARD WITH COVER OFF (YOU CAN FEED STRINGS THROUGH THE HOLES)

- STRING

- MARBLES

- BUBBLE GUM

- EMPTY CD CASE

- RULER AND PENCIL (TO MAKE A SEESAW)

- FUNNEL

- PING-PONG BALLS

- RAMP OR TUNNEL FOR MARBLES OR TOY CARS

These are just some of the ingredients that people have used to do this experiment. You don't have to use any of them, but they are all useful.

METHOD

1 You will be constructing a chain reaction using as many different ingredients as you can find—or get to work together.

2 Set up the ironing board (with its cover off) and tie two pieces of string to it so that they hang down almost to the floor.

3 Stick a marble to each lower end of string with a bit of chewed bubble gum.

4 Pull back on one string and let it swing toward the other. Untie the upper knot to raise or lower the string so that you get a direct hit.

5 When you've got that pair working, make a note of where and how far the second marble (the one that gets hit) swings. Stand the empty CD case there.

6 Now repeat step 4 so that you have the making of a chain reaction: Marble 1 hits marble 2, which knocks the CD case over. (Replace the ingredients in their original position.)

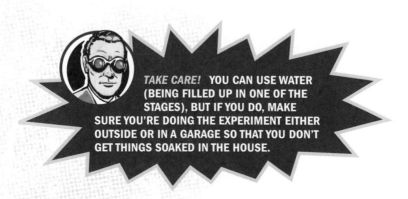

TAKE CARE! YOU CAN USE WATER (BEING FILLED UP IN ONE OF THE STAGES), BUT IF YOU DO, MAKE SURE YOU'RE DOING THE EXPERIMENT EITHER OUTSIDE OR IN A GARAGE SO THAT YOU DON'T GET THINGS SOAKED IN THE HOUSE.

7 Set up a seesaw made from a ruler balanced on a pencil so that the side hanging in the air will be hit by the CD case when it is knocked over. Repeat step 4 once again—now you have a new stage in the chain reaction.

8 Try to think of what you could put on the other side of the seesaw so that next time you'll have it sent into the air when marble 1 hits marble 2, which knocks the CD case over, which triggers the seesaw.

9 Continue adding stages to create an even bigger chain reaction, always noting where each element was.

The Scientific Excuse

A physicist would say that your experiment is all about "work," because energy has been transferred to an object—or a whole series of them. You provided the energy with your first push. Then it traveled down the line, transferring potential energy (the energy of something at rest) to kinetic energy (movement). A chemist would say, "Hmmm, I guess that experiment's not reversible." Because unlike some chemical experiments (like water freezing then ice melting), you can't run this one backward.

MUDDY WATER

THANKS TO RACHEL CARSON AND OTHER ACTIVISTS, PEOPLE are taking much more interest in protecting the environment. Banning DDT and other harmful chemicals, as well as controlling the amount of waste entering the air and water, has had an enormous effect. Many habitats have seen a return of plant and animal species that had been missing for decades. The numbers of walleye, an important food fish, are thriving once more in Lake Erie, which was always considered to be the most polluted Great Lake. And wild salmon have even begun swimming up the river Seine into Paris.

Those success stories are good examples of how nature can solve problems, if it is given a chance. As long as the flow of waste materials and pollutants is reduced or stopped, water can often clean itself.

This experiment shows how the water cycle—the constant cycle of evaporation (liquid water turning into water vapor, a gas) and condensation (the vapor cooling into liquid form again)—helps separate water from other materials. It works best on a warm, sunny day.

METHOD

1 Mix 2 cups of dirt or sand with 4 cups of water in the mixing bowl. Stir the mixture well.

2 Carefully put the drinking glass in the center of the bowl, easing it into the mixture but not letting the mixture into it.

3 Cut a length of plastic wrap about as long as it is wide, so that you have roughly a square shape.

4 Put the wrap over the opening of the bowl, but not too tightly. You must leave some slack.

5 Put the bowl in a sunny position, either by a window or outside, and place the marble on the wrap directly above the glass. (Because of the slack, the marble should rest neatly above it, enabling water to drip from it straight into the glass later in the experiment.)

6 Leave for several hours and then peel off the plastic wrap.

TAKE CARE! SOME PEOPLE FIND IT A BIT TRICKY GETTING THE PLASTIC WRAP SLACK OVER THE BOWL BUT TIGHT AROUND THE RIM. MAKE SURE YOU HAVE ENOUGH PLASTIC WRAP SO THAT YOU CAN HAVE TWO OR THREE GOES TO GET IT RIGHT.

7 You should find some clean water inside the glass and the sand or dirt mixture much drier. That is because the sun warmed the water, turning it into vapor. The vapor cooled slightly when it hit the wrap. It then condensed back into liquid and dripped down into the glass. The marble added enough weight to make the wrap dip—and the condensed water drip—in the middle, just above the glass. This water cycle occurs on a larger scale with oceans, lakes, or rivers supplying the water that evaporates and then cools (condenses) back into rain.

The Scientific Excuse

Most impurities in water—the dirt and sand in this case—get left behind when the water turns from liquid to gas by evaporating. That means that it remains pure when the vapor (water when it's a gas) cools and condenses back to liquid form. The evaporation–condensation process lies at the heart of the water cycle, which sends water from sea to sky to river to sea again. But the other feature—leaving the impurities behind—is the basis for many water-treatment schemes. Engineers can build systems so that waste water is evaporated and saved in pipes or other containers. Any dangerous or dirty material that remains can be collected and taken away.

Kitchen AVALANCHE

WHEN THEY'RE NOT DIGGING THEMSELVES OUT FROM TWO tons of snow, avalanche scientists use scaled-down models to predict the behavior of snow and ice in a wide range of circumstances. This experiment is a version of those models, using household items to take the place of ice, boulders, snow, and rough terrain.

It's best to do this experiment indoors, so that an unexpected gust of wind can't trigger the avalanche before you're ready. You'll be setting up four separate sets of avalanche conditions, arranged as four stripes of the same size across the foam-board base. If you're being really scientific, you'll have a pen and paper handy to identify each type and to record just what happened— and when—to each of those four.

TAKE CARE! ONCE YOU'VE GOT ALL FOUR CONDITIONS SET UP, IT'S REALLY IMPORTANT TO CONDUCT THE REST OF THE EXPERIMENT SLOWLY AND STEADILY. AFTER ALL, YOU'RE LOOKING FOR WHAT MIGHT BE VERY SMALL MOVEMENTS AT FIRST, AND YOU WANT TO BE ABLE TO NOTE JUST WHEN EACH OF THOSE OCCURRED.

You Will Need

- 36-INCH X 12-INCH PIECE OF FOAM BOARD (FOAM CORE)
- RULER
- PENCIL
- WAX PAPER
- SCISSORS
- BURLAP
- ABOUT 10 JELLY BEANS
- GLUE
- NEWSPAPER
- MATTER-RETAINING MEASURING CUP
- 2 CUPS GRANULATED SUGAR
- 5-POUND BAG WHITE FLOUR
- 2 CUPS INSTANT MASHED POTATO FLAKES
- 4 PAPERBACK BOOKS OF THE SAME THICKNESS

DANGER
AVALANCHE

1 Divide the foam board into 4 equal parts. First, measure out and mark dots at 9 inches, 18 inches, and 27 inches along the long sides of the foam board. Then, use a pencil to connect these dots so that you wind up with four 9-inch-wide by 12-inch-long panels. It should look like this.

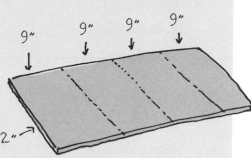

2 Cut a 9-inch by 12-inch strip of wax paper and an identical strip of burlap.

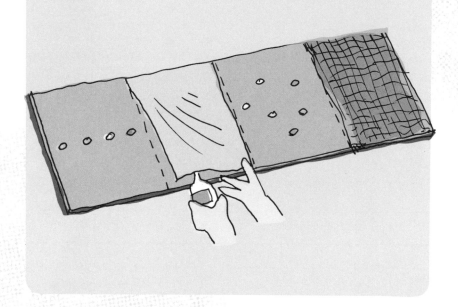

3 Glue 4 jelly beans in a line halfway across (that is, roughly 6 inches down) the left-hand panel (the first on the left) and glue the rest of the jelly beans randomly across the third panel.

4 Glue the wax paper to the second and the burlap to the fourth panel.

5 Give the glue time to dry.

The Scientific Excuse

This experiment is an ideal introduction to one of the tools that scientists and engineers depend on—modeling. The best way to study or predict actions is to observe them firsthand. But it's not possible to do that most of the time: Imagine trying to measure Antarctica's ice caps or the flow of the Amazon in a lab! That's why it's important to create models, usually on a much smaller scale, to create similar circumstances. In this case, those circumstances are the different types of snow falling on a mountain. Scientists and engineers study models like this one and apply their conclusions to real life. That transfer to the wider world is called "extrapolation."

6 Spread the newspaper on the table or counter where your avalanche will take place and set the prepared foam board on it. It should be level at this point, with the prepared side facing up.

7 Shake some granulated sugar over the entire foam board: This represents the first winter snowfall.

8 Sprinkle half of the flour (representing heavy snowfall) over the entire surface, covering the sugar completely, and pat it all down evenly.

9 Now sprinkle a layer of instant mashed potatoes (representing light dry snow in the coldest part of winter) over everything.

10 Finally, sprinkle the remaining flour (heavy snow in milder, windier conditions) over everything, and pat down evenly.

11 You now have an avalanche waiting to happen.

12 Carefully lift one of the long edges of the foam board and slide a paperback under it so that you create a slight slope. Observe any slips and other movement.

13 Carefully add more paperbacks one by one to increase the angle slope, noting which conditions are most (and least) stable.

14 With the tip of your pencil, tap lightly at various points on your slope. Can you spot where the most likely place for an avalanche will be?

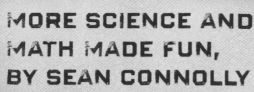